1

Spirit is the Divine Essence that exists within us, and of course all around us. That singular energy, that unity and oneness expresses itself in so many shapes and forms in such beauty and grace. The experience of expression is ecstasy, to be just one yet be able to see oneself, sense oneself, and hear oneself is divine. Each expression is a note, so unique and profound that no other expression can duplicate it. Each note is a song, never ending and captivating to all who can still themselves enough to hear it.

Where is the greatest joy? Can it be found in singing the song or in knowing the song has been heard by oneself? Can you imagine the perfect pitch of the soul when it finally recognizes itself once having been lost in between the movement of matter? Can you envision a place where every soul is singing freely it's song of existence? That place is deep within us and can be found. That song is waiting for us to sing. That heaven is waiting for us to arrive, to remember the chorus, the dream and the orchestra surrounding us.

We can remember our selves in this dance. We can choose to see another us and then create anew. Our world is a vision that we hold for ourselves in time and space. Our reality is a continuum of consciousness streaming and pouring out of the ocean. Embrace your song and you will hear how Spirit sings through each of us. As our songs never need end our separation never need begin. See yourself in the oneself. See your light in the Source, see your Divinity and know that we are the precious bringers of light, cascading out from waves of love.

These songs in your hand have been written by this soul Hal Manogue, but he has written it not for himself. He has captured the music he hears playing in the ethers and has

2

dedicated his life to reflecting the love he sees in every drop. He knows the Songs of Spirit must be heard, must be shared and freed. He knows and sings and shares and dances with delight at hearing Life's orchestra. These words are full of the compassion and inspiration that his soul wants reveal for all those he sees around him. Driven by the passion to help others hear the still sound of peace beating silently, he holds no barriers or boundaries. By immersing himself in the songs being heard he becomes an instrument, fine tuned and precise.

You have in your hand an instrument of peace, singing softly yet perfectly. You hold in your heart an instrument of love, beating gently yet never alone. As it beats it waits to hear the sound of Spirit. It waits to see it self, it waits patiently and full of confidence that the song can be found, and that the song can be sung. Let your limitations dissolve into the music, allow your mind to escape in the familiarity of the words, let your life expand into the infinity Hal's soul will take you to. Allow your self to experience this grace and know that it can never end. Let these songs take you beyond where you think you need to be, to within, to a heaven that awaits for only you to return so we can all live in the perfect and whole oneness from whence we came.Would you want it any other way?

Cherise Elizabeth Thorne
June 2008

To Cherise and all my Angels

Special Thanks

To the following publications for publishing works from this book:

New Age Tribune: www.newagetribune.com

Mystic Pop Magazine: www.mysticpopmagazine.com

Writers In The Sky: www.writersinthesky.com

Lightship News: www.star999@sbcglobal.net

EzineArticles.com: www.ezinearticles.com/

Seasons Of The Soul: www.seasonsofthesoul.com

Riehl Life: www.riehlife.com

Temple Of The Knowing Spirit: www.knowingspirit.com

Ascension Network: www.ascensionnetwork.com

A Secret Turning In Us

Makes The Universe Turn.

Head Unaware Of Feet,

And The Feet Head.

Neither Cares.

They Keep Turning.

Rumi

Note From The Author

The 2008 collection is the third in a series of ten works.
Each year brings change to my physical life. It brings even
more change to my consciousness. This work was written in the
early months of 2007, and it came out of thoughts of unity.
I have been striving to connect my focus consciousness with
other aspects of my other selves. When I try to do this, it
never works. Something brings me back to earth and life moves
along in an orderly chaotic fashion. But the early days of 2007
were a bit different; I did experience and feel other selves
expressing thoughts through my fingers. I didn't realize what
I was writing until I reread each poem, and saw a pattern
taking shape. The pattern was a doorway to other realities and
life forms. I still am at the doorway; but I am feeling that I have
more to me than meets the eye. (As my friend Yvonne says.)

As you read the works I think you will sense this change; this
switch of focus, and will understand that we all are much more
than we have been taught. Within our consciousness lie worlds
of indescribable life forms and foundations. Each world is
unique yet connected to a stream of consciousness that is
constantly changing and expanding.

I believe we will continue to remember these other selves and
they will enhance our physical lives in glorious ways. My journey
like yours is one of discovery and growth. We are here to be
grander versions of the spirit's we think we are, and to express
that grandeur in gratitude.

I hope you will feel that awareness as you read the poems.
It is by no means the end or the answer to anything; it is an
awakening that will continue in some form for eternity. We chose
the path, we experience.

Welcome to my path, I am on my way to 2009, but I am bringing
my now with me; leaving nothing, accepting everything and
changing constantly.

H.T.M.
Franklin Tennessee
December 2007

A Blue Print Of An Unknown Reality!

Webster's Dictionary defines a poem as: An arrangement of words written or spoken that express experiences, ideas or emotions in a style that is more concentrated, imaginative and powerful than that of ordinary speech or prose. Some poems are in meter, others in prose and others are in free style.

When I began writing poems I didn't read that definition. I didn't expect to spend my life writing a form of poetry that is to most that read it, a self-given poetic license. The poems I write do not fit into the recognized structure of poetry; they are hybrids of thought that are hard to understand in normal terms. Using accepted beliefs about the nature of my existence will not bring my work into focus. By releasing myself to another form of my consciousness I am able to verbalize that consciousness in a manner that is unique, yet similar.

This journey of awareness began early in life for me, but I repressed it and felt a great amount of fear when I realized the diversity that existed within me. I made the choice to live my life as a typical human, working, marrying, having children and being generally discontent in the circumstances that formed my life. I blamed this feeling on others and outside factors that did not want me to feel good about myself; it way easier to put the burden of unhappiness on something or someone else and continue living in fear and anger. I was able to judge others; I put myself on a table of right and wrong so that I could justify my actions. I was the fork that lifted the food of righteous- ness to my mouth and the knife that cut the unwanted fat of diversity from my plate. I was the spoon that swirled and dissolved the sugar of lies into my drink of anxiety. I sat at this table for almost forty years and then the table collapsed.

My mother died in 1996, and her death completely shattered that table into tiny pieces. I wanted answers about death; I wanted answers about sickness and I wanted answers about living. I began a new journey through time reading everything I could find about those topics and I found myself meeting someone I never expected to meet; another me. All the philosophy books, all the psychology books and the self help books from voices around the world lead me to a place that I had completely forgotten, called the unknown reality within me.

I found a blueprint of myself waiting for me to build a physical foundation of freedom in linear time. The blueprint had always been there wrapped in a corner of my mind waiting for me to feel it. I began to feel it through the words of Rumi the 13th century Sufi poet. I felt it through Rilke the 19th century German poet. Through other poets such as: Goethe, Blake, Dickinson, Takahashi, and Buson, the list is long. I found life after physical death in their words and I knew my mother was still alive and focused on another stream of her consciousness. In 1998 I began to write poetry and I write and live it everyday since my awakening. My blue print of consciousness has become a physical life.

My words come from that blueprint, and at times they are hard to understand with this focused consciousness, but at some point in time they begin to make sense. My purpose in this physical life is to experience the variety and complexity that physical consciousness gives me, so I can expand the other aspects of my self. My poetry is the vehicle that comes from the past, and is painted in the future so I can ride in my now. It is my spirit's song of love.

As I begin my yearly collection of Short Sleeves A Book For Friends (this is the third year) I do it with joy, gratitude and acceptance. I invite all of you to feel that blueprint; feel your unknown reality, by tasting mine. Yours will be different and diverse but it is as valid as mine is. Now is the moment for remembering and I offer my work as universal service to All There Is.

H.T.M.
2008

The Physical Story Of Ace

Someone once said:
"The mind is like a parachute, it only works when it's open".
As each day goes by I understand how true that statement is.

When I started writing my form of poetry,
I wanted to create a trademark or logo for my work.
I guess that desire came from all my years in the business world.

When I put my first book together in 2002, I needed something
for the cover that would help explain the work.
Since it was titled Short Sleeves A Book For Friends, I thought
a smiley face would work,
So I started with that concept and a figure emerged. The figure
started to take on a life of its own, within my mind.
I added stick arms and legs inside of pants and then a shirt, a
short sleeve shirt, and then realized it had to be a color,
But what color?

I was doing research on the human energy field at the time,
reading the workings of Barbara Ann Brennan
And others about our consciousness creating an energy field
that in turn creates the physical body.
Simply stated, the consciousness, the energy field and the
body are in a state of balance,
But when there is a change in consciousness caused by a decision
or reaction creating tension,
The energy field and the physical body will come into balance
with it and a symptom will appear as tension in the body reflecting
the tension in consciousness.
Part of the consciousness, the energy system, is composed of
seven energy centers called chakras (Meaning Wheel in Sanskrit).
The energy system is composed of different densities of
energy in a state of flow or movement.
When things flow smoothly we experience wholeness.

When energy is blocked we experience tension, which manifests as symptoms.
The charkas act as valves or pumps to regulate the flow of energy through the system.
The state of energy flow of consciousness is therefore determined by the chakras.
Each Chakra has a color associated with it. They are positioned from the sacral plexus in a straight line to the top of the head.
Each one has a color beginning with the lowest: Red, orange, yellow, green, blue, indigo and violet.
When functioning properly they are vibrant representations of those colors,
When energy is blocked they become distorted in color.

I had found the colors for my shirt. They would be the colors of the charkas.
In understanding that my consciousness was energy coming from somewhere and entering my body to become a human,
I drew a line of energy around my little friend with it entering at the feet and being released at the top of the head.
I also learned that there are other levels of energy less dense than charkas, called auras.
I represented one of them with a violet cloud surrounding my friend.
There he was all dressed up, but missing one important thing, a name.

I was looking at this new form grinning at what could be done with a smiley face and time on my hands
And the letters a c e popped into my head. A-c-e.
Yes, A for Aware; I was now aware that I am consciousness filled with energy, that has a mind and body.

C for Connected; this energy was coming from somewhere. I could call it whatever I wanted: God, Source, Universe, Source Self and that all names are OK. E for Energy; I was

aware and connected to life thru energy.
It flowed through me, around me and through all living things.
This energy is my consciousness and I am a whole part of
another whole, a collective consciousness that is the same
but diverse.
In understanding diversity I learn to be a grander version of my self.
Ace is a metaphor for consciousness;
He represents wholeness in body, mind and spirit.
He is waving at me, wanting me to remember who I am;
A spirit having a human experience.
He signifies the whole child within us all, inner truth connected
in joy and happiness to all there is,
Love.

About Ace

Facts About "Ace" Our Trademark

1. Ace stands for Aware Connected Energy.

2. Ace represents the unity we all have buried within us.

3. Ace is dressed in the colors of his charkas, all vibrant and healthy.

4. Ace is aware of his source and is an expression of that source.

5. Ace is connected to the universal stream of consciousness that flows through all life.

6. Ace is energy that pulsates in sync with his thoughts.

7. Ace is another aspect of the focused consciousness we have within us.

8. Ace is free from all the illusions that fear manifests.

9. Ace is love, filled with the power of All There Is.

10. Ace knows we are all one and he respects all life forms.

11. Ace lives in truth.

12. Ace follows his dreams and lives in the now.

13. Ace sees with his emotions and touches with his feelings.

14. Ace is the essence of gratitude.

15. Ace lives in abundance and shares his joy with a smile.

About Our Kids

Facts About The Kids; Our Other Trademark

1. Freedom, Awareness, Connection, Contrast are metaphors for our collective consciousness

2. Freedom has a will, a mind, and unlimited thoughts to create his world.

3. Connection is one with the universe and all life. She uses unity as the voice of the now.

4. Awareness feels other aspects of his consciousness and expresses them. He knows his higher self is there to assist him and guide him.

5. Contrast is everywhere and in all things. She is pure intention and perception. She is the symbol of growth and expansion.

6. The kids are in a field of energy that radiates love and joy. There have no opposite and rest in gratitude.

7. The kids know only peace and the spirit of consciousness.

8. They are pure energy in pure thought.

9. They are the consciousness before physical birth.

10. They are the consciousness after death.

11. They are what we are in the light of eternity.

12. They are the mirrors of life looking back at us.

13. They do without doing.

14. They watch their desires manifest into things.

15. They ask and it is given.

16

Table Of Contents

My World

Rippling Thoughts
Spot My World
With Impulses
Probabilities Surround Me
In
Electromagnetic Magic

Wonders
Of Creation
That Stand
Before Time
Sparkle
With Opportunities

In My World Of Growth
Science
Fails
To See Itself

Religion
Tests
Intuitiveness

Wisdom
Unwraps Itself
In Energy

I Become
All I Feel
In The Pot
Of Diversity
Boundaries
And Limits
Drop
From Sight

Awareness Lights
My Mental Passages
With Symbols
Of Connection

I Find
The Self
That Was
Never Lost
I Was
Only Misplaced

Epistemology

Chocolate Roses

Drip With The Fragrance Of Love

Mint laced Thoughts

Melt Into A Creamy Reality

Spicy Melodies Float On Clouds

Of Freedom

Bubbling Friendships Unite

In The Bottle Of Time

Tender Memories Swim

In The Waters Of Now

Delicious Dreams

Sizzle In The Drizzle

Of Polarity

Future Rides

On The Back

Of Present's

Epistemology

A Splash Of Energy

A Splash Of Energy
Creates
A World
Of Effervescence

Raging Spirals
Of Atom And Particles
Swiftly
Aligning Into Matter

Form And Substance
Become Symbols
Of Existence

Bodies Effuse
From Thought
In Efficient Masterpieces
Winds
Of Efficacious Knowledge
Whisper
In Elaborate Elasticity

Elders Become Children
In the Electricity Of Electrons
Elegant Elements
Of Consciousness
Elope In Grandeur
Embarking
With The Essence
Of Expansion

I Move Towards
The Center Of My Embryo
Emblazed In Unity
I Become One
Within Creation
Embosomed In Love
I Breath

Deep Valleys

Deep Valleys
Overflow With Life
Ocean's Mighty Test Tube
Awakens A World Of Silence
Rippling Water Mountains
Hold
The Catalyst
For Change

Relentlessly
On Their Shelves
Ageless Memories
Bring Whales to Shore
Dolphin's Play
In Magic Soup
Stirring Ancient Ingredients
With Consciousness

Rainbows
Of Fish Swim
In Aqua Marine Grandeur
Seeing Themselves
In Multiplicity

Fauna
Move In Vibrating Sequences
Whispering
In Synchronicity
Deep Secrets
Reveal Unity
Missing Links
Find Service Annoying
Never
Being Lost At All

Captive Angels
Smile
In Wisdom
A Boat
Of Oneness
Floats
In Eternity
Creatively

I Call Me

Imagination Inspires Me
To Perceive Beauty
Within
My Self

Glowing Memories
Of The Future
Beckon Me
To Shine

Changing Past Lives
Knock
At My Door
Of Awareness
Other Selves
Wait Patiently
Outside
Of My
Focused Perception
Ready
To Enhance
The Meaning
Of Life

My Source Self
Projects Me
In Particles
Of Energy
That Interact
With The Formula

Of Everything
I'm Completely Connected
To The Knowledge
Of The Ancient Creator
Who Is Born
In My Now

Opening
A Window
In My Closed Mind
I See My Self
As
A Multidimensional
Aspect
Of
An Extraordinary
Experience
I Call Me

I Want

Gentleness Rides
With Beauty
In Painted Colors
Of Life
A Glow
Of Peaceful Energy
Sits
Within Me

I See
The Beasts and Fauna
Duplicating Their Creator
In Harmony
In Sync
With Themselves
Without Doubt
Without Question
They Are
A World United
In Their Choices

I Want To Ride
In The Beauty
Of Nature

I Want To Paint Myself
With The Colors
Of Energy
That Rest
Within Me

I Want To Be
In Harmony
With My Creator
I Want To Be In Sync
With My Creation

I Want To Be United
In My World
Of Choices

I Want
My Thoughts
To Be
Your Thoughts
I Want Me
As You
Want Me

Without Question
Without Doubt
In The World
Of Oneness

Spirit's Song

Continuous Roots
Mesh
Within Me

Interlocking
Consciousness Awakens
To
The Sound
Of
Forgiveness

Ripening Seeds
Of
Desire
Fall Freely
Through
The Fertile Soil
Of Oneness
And
Plant Themselves
In Reality

Each
Self Dances
In Endless Harmony

Rotating Partners
Hold Patterns
Of
Remembering
Tightly
In Place

As The Wind
Of Change
Blows
Its Spirit Song
Through
The Tree
Of Life

I Taste
One Fruit
Of
Gratitude

And
One Sip
Of Life
In
The Cup
Of
Being Human

Proof

Prayer
Is Feeling Connected
To A Probability
Of Reality

Processions
Of Dreams
March Towards
Infinite Possibilities

Each Family
Of Consciousness
Is Fueled
By
Knowing

Constantly Changing
From One Perfection
To Another
A Cluster Of Consciousness Is
A Never Ending Source
Of Probabilities

An Energy Procured
In Profound Projections
Of Thought

Progressive
But Not Linear
Profane But Not Pagan

Proficient
In The Profusion
Of Knowledge
Progenitive
Without Programs

A Prophetic Projection
Of Parts
That Do Not Comprise
The Whole
Prolific
In Cruciferous Life

Proof That Prayers
With
Pronounced Vision
Of Unity
Is
Within Itself

Many Realities

Playful Focus
Brings Me Happiness
Special Thoughts
Of Learning
Travel Through
My Body

Internal Signals
Light My Path
And Peace
Surrounds Me

Lessons Remembered
Ring Out
In Pleasure

Simple Smiles
Turn To Laughter
Energy Gushes
Through My Pores
And Displaces
Doubt

Sincerity Radiates
Simplicity Dominates
Love Celebrates
In Ecstasy

Consciousness
Feels
Universality
In
Many
Realties

Real

Real
Is
A Room
Where I Stand
Wearing
Nothing
But
My Self

Real
Is
Just One Me
In
The House
Of
Multidimensionality

I Feel
The Sap
Of Consciousness
Stretch
Within Me

I Hear
The Sounds
Of Nature
And
I Awaken
From

A
Sleep
I See
The World
Changing
And My Body
Skips
A
Beat.

I Catch
A Sunburst Butterfly
And
Feel Its Beauty
Rests
In
Me.

IT

Consciousness
Is Timeless
It
Moves Faster Than
The Speed
Of Light

It
Is
In All Life

It
Is Not Divided
Or Split
But Flows
In Aspects
Of Itself

It
Is
A System
Of Codes
Generating Different Realities
Simultaneously

It
Has No Laws
But It Is Freedom
Of Expression
And Attraction

It
Is Spirit Along
With Form
Innate As
Well As Infinite

It
Fills Space
With Life
And Life
With Space

It
Has Memory
Meaning
And Motivation
Complete In Itself
Yet
Not Complete
In Diversity

It's
Unity
Is Creativity
Its Soul Is Eternal
Its Energy Is Within Me
Around Me
And Is Me
It's Connection
It's Direction
Is
All There Is
Love

Expressing Itself
In The Power
Of The Now
Graciously
I Find Myself
And
It

United Colors

Rooted Within Me
Are The Colors
Of My Spirit
Spinning Cordellas
Of Energy
Seeking Expression

The Light Switch
Of Thought
Turns Me
Into
A Rainbow
That Curves Back
Into Consciousness

I Express Myself
In Health
In Wealth
In Fear
Building A Physical Model
That Projects Itself
In The Daily Illusion
Of Drama
I Call Life

Unaware
That I Am
Seven Charkas
Filled With Wholeness

I Wander Thru My Mind
Looking Everywhere
But Within
To Cure
The Agony
I Create
For Myself

My True Prescription
For Wellness
Waits
For Me
Within My World
Of United Colors
That Are Eager
To Heal Me

All They Need
Is Me
Thinking
Open
Mindedly

Simple Me

To Be A Tree

Simple Me

Let Me Be Thee

Said The Flea

Prayer

Our Free Will
Builds Shrines
To Kneel Before
And Pray

Prayer
Is Connection
Of Consciousnesses

Consciousness Creates
Thoughts
Thoughts Become
Matter
Matter Has
Energy

Energy
Is Awareness
Of Being

Being
Is A State In Emptiness
Emptiness
Is Filled With Love

Love
Is Infinite Knowing
And Appreciation
The Nature
Of Knowing
Is Light
Light
Appears From Darkness
So That
All Prayers
Are Answered

My Bucket Of Time

Like The Waterfall
I Plunge
Into Myself

Rays
Of Light
And
Voices
Of Energy
Surround Me

I Capture My Essence
In High Definition
Consciously Moving In Harmony
With
My Density

I Color My Aura
With Crayons
Of Thought

Each Filled
With Healing Tones
That Form A Body
Of Health

I Swim
In The Waters
Of Universal Life
Resting
On The Shores
Of Gratitude
I Kiss
The Wind
Of Awareness

Holding
The Sand
Of Connection
In My Bucket
Of Time

A Whole Of Me

Ever-Present Inner Worlds
Are Physically
Rooted
In Thought

Twisted DNA
Unravels
In The Movement

Tunnels Of Energy
Supply
Vitality To Dreams
In
An Under Toe
Of Reality

Long Challenged Ideas
Spring Into Motion
Capping Mountains
Of Doubt With Truth
Synthetic Gestures
Drown In Pools
Of Belief

Armies
Of Angels
Are Dressed For Peace
Flowing Gowns
Of Freedom
Cover My Mind

Heaven Absorbs Hell
In Self Knowledge
Locked Doors
Open
With Majestic Ease
Cracked Floors
Shine With Celestial Smiles
I Sit
On Nature's Knee
Watching Consciousness
Make
A Whole
Of Me

Conglutination

Being A Better Thought
I Flower In A Wilderness
A Cactus
Of Belief
Stands Tall
Within Me

My Sandstone Mind
Awakens With Color
As My Sky Dances
In Fullness
Mental Photos
Paint
The Sunset
In Hues
Of Splendor

Standing
On A Cliff
Of Passion
Nature
Brushes My Shoes
With Life

My Heart Soaks
In Desire
Hearing My Spirit's
Laughter
Sheepish Luck
Kneels In Prayer
In The Church
Of Illusion

Wolves Of Mercy
Disappear In Collusion
Collective Consciousness
Collides With Itself
In Colure

The Coma
Of Wellness
Combust
In Comedy

The Comity
Of Union
Is My Commissary
Of Dreams

Common Knowledge
Becomes
An Infinite
Commodity
Colorfast
Is My Vision
Of
Conglutination

My Violet Chakra

My Violet Chakra Opens
With A Kiss
From
Infinity
My Consciousness
Is Painted
In Multidimensional Art

Colors
Of Unknown Vibrations
Fill My Chamber
Of Understanding
With Crystal Images
Of Forgotten Lives

Chaos
Is A Changeable Chapel
Of Learning
A Chapbook
Of Formlessness
That Shapes My Charade
In An Oven
Of
Character

Reaching
For The Charcoal Pencil
Within Myself
I Chart A Course
Already Taken
But
Now Remembered

Pulling My Chariot
Of Freedom
Is A Self
Of Splendor

Parking In The Chateau
Of Clairvoyant Images
My Painting Sits
In The Reality
Of Diffusion
Digesting
Itself In
Awareness

I Watch God

Reaching Out
From Within
Brings Me Closer
To My Self

Feeling Love
Encircle My Form
Connects Me
To The Riches
Of Being Human
All I Have
Is
For All To Share

In Giving
And Receiving
I Have No Limits
No Walls
Or Fences
To Hinder
My Growth

My Truth
Stands
In The Great Nest
Of Thoughts
Then Flies
Through The Universe
To An Infinite Galaxy
Of Energy
Where I Watch God
Comb His Hair
In A Eternal Stream
Of Consciousness

Only Just Begun

A Grand Music Plays Within Me
A Choir Of Connected Voices
Move Through Me
Visions Of Reality Pulsate In Harmony
A Performance In Consciousness
Flows Freely

Unimaginable Becomes Imaginable
Walls Of Fear Dissipate
And I Announce My Birth In Sounds
Not Heard But Felt

I Open Myself To Each Note
I Feel The Oneness
Of Connection
Wrapping Myself
In The Web Of Every Clef
Slavery Stops Playing
In The Breathless Air

Dancing
In The Garden Of Awareness
With Nothing
But Gratitude
I Sense The Melody
Has Only Just Begun
To Be
Me

Tango Of Infinity

Mystery
Dances Before My Eyes
My Perspectives Twist
In New Found Thoughts
My Perceptions Turn
Into New Horizons
Where Illusions Waltz
From Sight
And Reality
Becomes Multidimensional

Cadent Vibrations
Harmoniously Whisper
In Free Flowing Melodies
Gently Awakening
My Dormant Emotions
With Opportunities
Of Enlightenment

The Mystery
Untangles Itself
On The Dance Floor
Of My Mind
Antiquity Embraces My Spirit
And Wraps Itself
In The Arms
Of Creation
In
The Tango Of Infinity

No Time

Electromagnetic Energy
Collides With My Thoughts
To Create Matter
A Body
A Poem
A Building
A World
A Universe

Each Thought
Or Desire
Is Manifested
In Form
Looking Around My World
I See Opportunities
For Growth
I Feel The Pull
Of Other Realities
Simultaneously

Reincarnation
Is Happening Now
As I Experience
This Physical Me
These Words
Are The Transmitter
Of Camouflaged Information

Releasing Myself
To A Grander Illusion
Of Being
I Absorb
The Building Blocks
Of Life
In The Context
Of Multidimensional Presence

The Wisdom
Intuitively Resting Within
Opens
In The Fantastic Splendor
Of Limitlessness
No Longer Caged
In A Prison Of Sin
I Escape
Into Myself
And Feel
The Gift
Of
No Time

My Ice Mountain

My Ice Mountain
Is Melting
Frozen Thoughts
Are Transformed
Into Crystals
Of Being

Mental Blocks
Formed By Ignorance
Are Freely Dripping
Into Unity

Three Dimensional Senses Are Joined
By Multidimensional
Awareness
Streams Of Intuitive Knowledge
Fill Me
With Connection

Mysterious Rock Formations
Speak With Clarity
New Life Vibrates
In Clarion Clearness
Classic Fears
Drown In Clarification
Claves Beat
In Clandestine Fashion

My Soul Snaps Free
Of A Claustrophobic Closet
Of Self Absorption
Into A Lake Of Clairvoyant Tranquility
Warmed By Possibilities
Found In Endless
Cisterns
Of
Creation

Infinite Confirmation

At Sunrise and Sunset
A Door Opens
A Wormhole
Where My Consciousness
Flies
To Destination Known
Yet Forgotten

Expanded Thoughts
Of Unity
Congeal In Fluid Love
Congenital Spirits
Are Confluent

Confident Configurations
Attract
The Essence
Of Creation
In The Purity
Of Being

Pulsating Energy Vibrates
Through My Body
My Soul Sees Itself
In Wholeness
The Wind Whispers
The Sea Dances
Eternity Forms A Rainbow
Of Blessings

Congeries
Of Gifts
Shared In Conformity
Awaken My Life
Of Conflict
To Infinite
Confirmation

Drifting

Drifting
In A Boat Of Dreams
My Thoughts Row
Through Waves
Of Anxiety
Seeking To Find
The Shore Of Wholeness

Rocks Filled
With Yesterday's Fears
Block My View

Caught In The Current
Of Acceptance
I Row In Circles
My Mind Lost
In Search Of Itself

Darkness Covers
My Hope Of Success
Conformity Holds My Desire
In An Anchor
Of Loneliness

Suddenly
A New Wave Of Thought
Sinks My Boat
I'm Cast
Into An Altered State
Where White Caps
Of Love
Push Me Upward

I Find Myself Floating
In The Mist
Of Another Reality

A Connected Consciousness
Is Kissing My Lips
I Taste
The Salt Of Oneness
Filling
My Lifeless Body

Another Wave
Washes
Over My System
Of Narrow-Mindedness
Cleansing And Clearing
My Trapped Vision
Releasing Me
From
Distorted Perceptions

A Bright Light
Of Belief
Warms My Body
My Skin Vibrates
With Energy
Now
I See Myself
As A Wave
That Carries Me
To A Sea
Of
Universal Consciousness

Simple Awareness

Beneath My Surface
Lies
A World Of Dreams
That Rest
In Complete Freedom

Digging Within Me
I Feel My Other Selves
Filled With
The Energy Of Love

I'm Covered
In The Warmth Of Unity
Knowing
There Is More To Me
Than Force Filled Traditions
And
Distorted Beliefs

Rejoicing In Discovery
My Focused
Self Jumps
Into My Illusion
With New Vision

Answering
Old Question
With
New Thoughts

Kissing
My
Collective Consciousness
With
Lips
Of Remembering
I Grow
In The Simple Awareness
Of
Synchronicity

Purls With Pleasure

Reaching
To Feel Myself I Dream
Without Dreaming
I Know Without
Knowing

Intense Wisdom
Circles My Psyche
Psalmodies
Of Color And Shape
Arrange My Thoughts
In Pubescence Ptosis
Brings Me
To
Awareness

Psychometric Connections
Abound
In Private
Publicity

Puffs
Of Unity
Pulsate
In Atomic Fashion
Puissant Forms
Pump Energy
With Pundit Beauty
My Pupa Explodes
In Purpose
I Am Purified
In Plurality
Purine Love
Purls
With Pleasure

My Course In Miracles

Being Totally Connected
But Unaware Of My Self
I March Through Life
Covered In Mystery

Searching For Answers
Brings More Questions
Completely Surrounded By Knowing
I Fall Asleep In Its Gentleness

Dreams Make Me Understand
The Complexity
Of Consciousness
I Live In Several Realities
Simultaneously
But Focus On One

Binders Of Misinformation
Restrict My Belief
In Unity

Fragments Of Myself
Are Throw About Like Confetti
Celebrating Integration
With Nothing

Swirling Particles Of Matter
Capture
My Design
And I Set Sail On The Ship
Of
Forgetfulness

Floating In A Stream
Of All There Is
I Lift My Spirit
From The Galley
Of Separation

Sails
Of Eternity
Wave
In The Wind
Of Love

My Course
In Miracles
Arrives
Where It Never Left
In The Web
Of The Divine Matrix
Of
Infinity

Love

Love
Speaks A Different Language
It Has No Country
Of Origin
No Dictionary
Filled With Symbols
It Is Not Black
Or White
Or Controlled
By Polarity Poles
Or Waves Of
Electromagnetism

It Rides Freely
In The Flow
Of Consciousness
Always Present Ready
And Able
To Be What I Am
Following
And Leading
Shaking
But Never Breaking
Surrounding
And Protecting
The Essence
That Is Me

Somehow
I'm Remembering
The Basic Part
Of Me
That Is Universality
Its Form Is Free
A Floating Star
A Golden Tree
Put Inside
Dimensionality

Hitch A Ride

Waves Of Energy
Break
On The Shore
Of Doubt

Returning
To My Beach
Of Loneliness
I Find Shells
Of Yesterday
Filled With Grains
Of Self Pity
White Dunes
Of Solitude
Surround Me

A Wind Of Remembrance
Dances In My Hair
My Feet Sink
In The Abundant
Wet Sand

I Feel
The Salty Sea
Of Forgiveness
Dripping Down My Legs
And Rays
Of Sunlight
Paint My Face Red
Earth's Color
Of Belief
I Follow My Shadow
To A Pier
Of Hope
My Eyes Meet
An Indigo Sky
And I Smile
At Traveling Clouds
On Their Journey
Back Home
To
Oneness

It's
Called My Time
To
Hitch A Ride

Covered In Joy

Instant Love
Needs No Word
For Creation
Infinity Dresses Itself
In Unity

Thought Brings Energy
Free Will
Brings Unity
To Diversity

Awareness Intersects
With
Consciousness
In A Display
Of Life

Seekers Find
What's
Never Lost
In A Cycle
Of Growth

Matter Forms
In Thought
Existence
Has No End
Logos
Has No Beginning

Illusions
Find Themselves
In Truth
Reality Lives
In Dimensions
Dreams Rest
In Wisdom
I Create Myself
In Mirrors
Of Connection
Covered
In Joy

Beauty

Beauty Is Omnipresent
Waiting
For Me
To Feel It

Then It Disappears
In Thoughts
Of Loneliness

Beauty Surrounds My Body
Waiting
For Me
To Feel It

I Try To Grab It
Only
To Find
Frustration

Beauty Flows
From The Sea
Of Eternity
Waiting
For Me
To Feel It

I Try To Drink It Only
To Find
The Dryness

Beauty Captures
My Heart
Waiting
For Me
To Be It

I Try To Free It
Only To Find
Illusion

Beauty Is My Thoughts
Waiting
For Me
To Be
Every Aspect
Of
Me

Applauding

The Roar
Of Oneness
Shatters
My Emotions

Aligning Myself
With Freedom
Brings
A Mystical Aura
To Life

Perceptions Gather Specks
Of Unity
Packing Them
Into
Beams
From
The Core
Of My Source

No Longer Plagued
With False Gods
I Dance
On The Stage
Of Forgiveness

Applauding
The Audience
For
My Unending Desire
To Be My Self
I Smile

A Wake

A Stream Of Consciousness
Rides
The Wave Of Love
To A Shore Of Individuality
With
Gentle Conviction

Each Shore Changes
In The Sand Of Eternity
Specs Of Shells
Filled With Infinite Energy
Seem Hidden
But
Are Clearly Present

Tiny Forms Of Gratitude
Swell Into Being
Compassionate Emotions
Of Life
Are Born In Freedom
And Dress
In Suits Of Armor
To Remember
How To Swim

Drowning
Just To Catch The Wave
That Never
Left The Shore
The Sweet Taste
Of Sea Water
Soaks In My Thoughts

United Groups
Of Circling Selves
Fly In
The Under Breeze

A Learning Heart
Pumps In Pure Gifts
Wrapped
Within An Echo
Delivered
By Another Shore

Floating
In A Salty Core
In Natural Cycles
That I Make
My True Self
Becomes
A Wake

Within Me

The Meaning
Of Life
The Nectar
Of Desire
Flows Around Me
Through Me
And
Is Me

Atoms Pulsate
In Patterns
And
Rhythms
Forming
Simultaneous Realities

My Consciousness Awakens
In Non Linear Shapes and Colors
Emerged
In Creative Probabilities

Procreating A Proclitic Prize
Of Multidimensional Existence
Prismatic Blue Prints
Of Pristine Principles
Explode

Primordial Clocks
Spin In Cycles
Of Prayer

Latent Circuits
Escape
In A Privilege Prerequisite
Of Knowing
A Presidium
Of One
Is Present
Within Me

Habit

Infinity's Direction
Moves In The Perception
Of Molecules
Inward Sight
Is Blinded
By Noise

Rain Spreads
Wisdom
Speaking With
The Voice
Of Thunder

Glacier's Drip
Through Rock
To Reunite In Beauty

Ocean's Create
Beaches
To Feast
In Foam

Melodies Drift
Through Mountains
To Hear
An Echo

I Chase Myself
For A Glimpse
Of Duplicity

Words Fool Themselves
With Symbols
Of Life

Consciousness Repeats Itself
In Multi Shades
Of Dimensions

Mystery
Has No Form
In Dreams

Creation
Is Expanding
To Know Itself

Love
Is Unequally Whole
In Its Parts

Death
Smiles
In The Birth
Of Unity

Freedom Knows

Instant Gratification
Abounds
In Thoughts
Of Giving

Loneliness
Is Non Existent
In Truth

Belief Has Faith
That Gives Birth
To Matter

Strength Rests
Firmly
Within
Itself

Words
Sit Quietly
In Feats
Of Splendor

Perfection
Is An Act
In Progress

Abundance
Has A Group
Mentality

Nature Expands
Within
It's Roots

Blossoms
Scent Themselves
In Beauty

Wisdom
Finds A Seat
In Eternity

Love
Is All That
Freedom
Knows

Another Me

Another Me Living A Dream
Opens
A Threshold

Lost Intentions Sleep
In Doorways
Mystical Allies
Have Grand Inventions

Tapping Freely
Into The Icy Waters
Of Change
I Move
In Synchronicity
With Feelings

Balls Of Space
Become Planets
Of Action

Powered
By The Energy
Within Me
Emphatic Symbols
Color Themselves
As Molecules

Reason
Falls Off The Edge

Of Science
Landing
In The Soup
Of Belief

Memories
Are Future Lives
Consciousness
Sits In Infinity

Smiling
On The Scale
Of Weightlessness
I Kiss
Another Me

Empowered

Invisible Grids
Of Energy
Become Visible
In
Consciousness

Solar Storms
Engulf My Thoughts
They Change My Mind
To Conform
With
My New Density

Free Flowing Life
Charges My Cells
With Ancient Messages
Clusters
Of Nebula
Fill Me
With
New Born Stars

A Galaxy
Of Grandeur
Unfolds
Within Me

A Self-Packed
In Other Selves
Floating
From
Universe
To Universe
Without
A Time Frame

Connected
With Infinity
In A Field Of Dust
Escaping Nothing
Releasing Everything
Accepting Oneness
Empowered
By The Impetus
Of Love
I Blink

I Pinch Myself

Digging Through Subjective Realities
Dreams Awaken
A New Era
No Longer Captured
By Conformity
I Travel Unabated

Worlds In Motion
Beckon Me
Each Layer Of Mystery
Perceives Itself

University
Becomes
Multiversity

Murmurs
Of Existence
Muse
In The Music

Mutations
Of Selves
Fly In Freedom

History
Is Muzzled
In Myth
I'm
Released
In Myraidical
Awareness

Then
I
Pinch Myself

Slowly Tapping In

Reflections
Of Candor
Shimmering
Specs
Of Healing
Clear
My Consciousness

Rippling Thoughts Of Karma
Bring Breaking Waves
Of Evolution
That Drench
My Body
In Peace

Standing Face To Face
With My Illusions
I See Myself
In A Mirror
Alone
But Surrounded
By Other
Realities

Spirit's
Gently Nudging Me
To Play
My Music
With The Band
And Dance
To The Beat
Of Unity

I Sing
A Song
Of Whispers
Slowly Tapping In
To My Thoughts

My Simple Notes
Of Gratitude
Take Me
For A Spin

Life
Is So Visible
Playing Music
Without Sin

Diversity

Connected Brushes Of Life
Paint A Portrait
Of Diversity
Each Life Brings
A New Thought
A New Experience
To The Canvas
Of Lessons

A Deep Desire Bubbles
In The Brushes
A Yearning To Be Whole
Within The Whole
Of The Portrait

An Integrated Spirit
Brings Expressive Union
And Vivid Colors
Of Change
To The Observer
As Well As
The Observed

In The Now
Life's Painting
Hangs Perfectly
In The Museum
Of My
Consciousness

A Wave

Within My World
Sits A Lake Of Pain
Flowing
Into A River
Of Acceptance

I Am
The Dam
That Holds The Lake
I Release Energy
With Each Thought
Or
I Contain It

Observing
The Lake Changes It
My Consciousness
Can Move The Lake
To The River
Changing The Course
Of
My Life

The Lake
A Remembrance
The River My Now

Each Drop
From The Lake
Showers

My Awareness
Each Molecule
From The River Drowns
Me In Connection
I Am
The Changing Waters
Of Intensity

A Wave Of Infinity
Hitting
The Shore Of Love
With
Magical Thoughts
I Believe
In Myself

A Form Of Matter

Rooted In Love There Is No Duality
The Seer
And The Seen
Are One

The Doer
And The Object
Are One

Self Nature
Sees Itself As One
One Is
The All There Is

Complete
But Expanding
Perfect
But Imperfect

Diverse In Discernment
Webbed In Energy
Fueled By Infinity
Nestled In Creativity
I Feel Alive
In Consciousness

I'M
A Form Of Matter
That Repeats Itself
In Universal
Thought

Each Other

In Gratitude
We Become
The Giver
And
The Receiver

In Love
We Become
The Gift

In Beauty
We Become
Diverse

In Truth
We Become
Whole

In Light
We Become
One

In Life
We Become
Each Other

Howling In Relief

Searching For Meaning
In Mystery
I Find Myself
Where
I Never Looked
Within

Outward Shadows
Play A Foolish Game
Of Death
Inheritance
Of Glory
Fades In Distortion

Question Rivet Me
To Useless Toil
Emptiness
Rambles
At
The Speed Of Light
Finding A World
Of Desires

Rich Voices Razz My Thoughts
Producing
Clarity
Of Being

Sincere Longings
Wrap Around Each Other
Forming
A Figment Of Silence
That Opens
With Verse

Afterthoughts Disappear
In Fruitful Knowledge
Every Action
Is A Token
Of Joy
Staring
At The Moon
I See Me

Howling In Relief
My Consciousness Moves
To Another Table
To Write

Grand Alignment

My Hidden Selves
Appear
When Clouds
Of Forgetfulness
Vaporize

Worlds
Of Different Densities
Interact
In An Evolving
Web
Of Life

Suffering
Is Released
Into The Shadows
Of A Dynamic Cycle
Of Wordlessness
Where
It Has No Meaning

I Move
From Grid To Grid
Filled
With Grand Alignment
Of Spirit

Touching Others
With Desire
As I'm Touched
With Energy
My Selves Pulsate
In The Oneness
Of
Infinite Being

In Splendor

Creation Speaks
Of Consciousness
In Color

Magnificence Forms
That
Fill Space

Visible Motion
Defines But One Reality
Non- Visible Life
Attracts Intuition
With Magnetic Hues
Of Inner Worlds

Emptiness Does Not Exist
In The Structure
Of Life

Events
Blend
With Perceptions
In The Melody
Of Feeling

Uniqueness
Of Spirit
Imprints Itself
On
The Universal Wall
Of Being
A Signature Pressed
In The Annuls
Of Infinity

Ever-Expanding
Ideas
Float Through
Wafer-ness
To Explode
In Thought

Energy Reshapes Itself
In
Marvelous Grandeur
To Express Oneness
In Diversity

Inner Worlds
Transport Time
To A Field Of Dreams
Where
Mystery Fades
As
Consciousness Paints
Itself
In Splendor

Release Me

Release Me
Let Me Turn
The Key
Of Thought

Let Me Walk
Thru My Closet
Of Dreams
And Dress Myself
In Rainbows

Let Me Jump
From Star To Star
And
Hip Hop
To The Moon

Let Me Run Naked
Covered With
The Love
Of Freedom

Let Me See Myself
As I Am
A Beam
Of Complete Energy
Void
Of Nothing
But
Filled With Everything

Egglessly

Creation's Mind
Fills
A Void
Simultaneously

Particles Move Faster
That Light
Consciousness
Continues To Expand
Within All life

In Order To Know Myself
I Must Sense
My Other Realities
I Must Fondle
My Awareness
In Joy
And
Enlighten
My Physical Being
With Truth

The Shackles
Of Being One Me
Drop
As I Wander
Through My Dreams

Speakers Edit
Without Concern
Listeners Absorb
Ecumenically
Emanating Waves
Of Energy
Frolic In Unison

Concrete Fixtures
Reconfigure
in Silence

Age Effaces
Effortlessly
Efflorescence Is Educed
With Effusion
My Ecospecies
Is
An Echelon
Within Me
That Effluxes
Egglessly
In Synchronicity

Before Me

Integrated Forms
Within Me
Move Mountains
Of Questions
To Valleys
Of Answers

These Valleys
Are Within
The Mountains
Complete Forms
Yet Incomplete
In Themselves

The Answers Are
The Questions
Joined
In A Bond
Of Unity

Capped By
The Snow
Of Truth
Ancient Laws
Of Attraction
Bring Me
To A Stream
Of Connection
That Runs Through
My Consciousness

Each Question
Is Answered
By A Different Self
A Different Form
That Is Aware
Of Its Source
By Knowing Itself

Running Through
The Mountains
Of My Mind
I Find
A Valley
Of Selves
Before Me

I Stand

Sitting
On The Bank
Nothing Swims Before Me
Waves
Of Energy Ripple Within
The Fullness

The Moon
Pulls Covers Over Its Face
As The Sun's Shadow
Shaves
In Darkness

Particles
Of Thought
Come Together
In Past Galaxies
Where
History Sleeps
In Freedom

Missed Memories Grab
The Spotlight
And Kiss A Whisker
With Gratitude

No Longer Trapped
In Mind Tornados
A Dream Forms

Of Servitude
It Appears
In Serpentine Rocks
Of Splendor

Sequels Of Sequins
Vibrate
In A Speechless
Sermon

Sequestered Images
Unite In Serenity
I Stand
In Infinity

Expanding Senses

Floating Memories
Lift Me
To The Universal
Wholeness
Of Life

Remnants
Of Deep Footprints
Washed Away By Tides
Of Forgetfulness
Linger Within Me

Self-Induced
Aggression
Challenges Me
To Sit
On A Beach
Of Dreams

Watching My Life
Ebb And Flow
With The Tide
Braking Waves
Of Energy
Split
By Yesterdays Wisdom
Reunite
In An Ocean
Of Catechism

Melting
Into A Sea Of Mythology
That Encapsulates
My Consciousness
In Vibrating Harmony
I Expand My Sense
Of Awareness
And Smile

By Pie

Raindrops
Of Eternity
Fill My Memory
While Distant Friends
Dabble In Dreams
Foreign Features
Film
A Life Saga

A Gentle Energy
Soaks My Mind

Colored Lenses
Capture
Multiple Journeys

Seeing Only Time
Throws My Symbols
Into Another Orbit
That Waffle
In Space

Creation
Lights More Worlds
Than One Round
Moving Rock

Skipping
Through Myself
I Feel
The Power
Of Laughter
The Glory
Of Forgetfulness
The Essence
Of Faith
In
A Shapeless Form
That Captures
Itself
In Joy

Endless Lines
Wrap In Circles

Standing
In The Middle
I Am
The Area
In Multiplicity
Surrounded
By Pie
My Radius
Is Squared

Off Key

Unity Blends
Without Sound
A Magic Mixture
Without Judgment
Flickering Ideas
Meld Into Dreams
To Become Reality
In Forms
Of Matter

Golden Memories
Become Life
In Mystic Auras
Peace Parades
Through Time
Carrying
Forgotten Selves

A Trumpet
Plays Unknown Music
As Centuries
Repeat Themselves

Corny Phrases
Light
The Meadows Of Reason
With Myths
Only To Redefine Life
In Comic Relief
Searching Elves
Sit On The Doorstep
Of Physical Wealth
Dumping
Their Harvest
With Laughter

Genders Reverse
In A Dance Of Remembering
Stoic Forms
Melt In Probabilities
Dripping Molecules
Cover Faults
With Intense Melodies
Sung Off Key

Diversity Kisses
Itself
In Forgiveness
While Energy Plugs
Another Hole

Brush Stroke

Dazzling Perceptions
Retrieve Reality
In An Symphony
Of Matter

Creativeness Rests
Within
The Reach
Of Thought
Flashing Intention
Surround Probabilities
A World
Awakens With Desire

Life
Is Not By Chance
Belief Showers
Opportunity
With The Wisdom
Of Consciousness

No Longer
Victimized By Fables
I Create Myself
In Richness

I Walk
With Angels
I Talk
To Beauty
In Rhythms
Of Unity

I Am
A Brush Stroke
Of Infinity

A Rock Of Love

Spiraling Through
The Mist
A Ray Of Light
Reflects
My Spirit

Intertwined
In The Union
Strands Of DNA
Untangle And Vibrate
Connecting Me
To A Fluid Consciousness
That Soars Past
The Speed Of Light
And Enters
A World Within Me

Time And Space
Dangle Outside
Waiting
For My Arrival

Planets
Call The Stars
In Search Of Yesterday
Future Galaxies
Wait Patiently
For Creation
The Moon
Slowly Moves
Towards The Rear

And The Sun Reloads
To Fuel My Dream
Awakened
By The Light
I Open Myself
With Gratitude
And Fly
To The Depths
Of Infinity
Landing
On A Rock Of Love
I Call Home

In Full Bloom

In Silence
The Wind Energizes
My Thoughts
Fresh Visions
Surround Me

The Will
To Grow
Brings Flavor
To Life
Ancient Wisdom
Intersects
With New Birth

A Comedy
Of Delight
Performs In Daylight
At Night
The Trumpets
Of Angels
Signal Freedom

I Float
With The Breeze
Catching Scenes
Of Myself
Switching From Captive
To Captor
A Mist

Drenches Me
In Awareness
No Longer Bound
By Mystery
I Become A Group
With The Force
Of One

Moving
Into Another Dream
A Field Of Creativity
Waits
To Be Discovered

Flowers
Of Unity Blossom
In Constant Change

In Full Bloom
I
Dance

Web Of Moments

Connected
Within Herself
She Moves
In Freedom
Wings Spread Across
The Canyon Of Souls

A Stream Of Cells
Packed In Feathers
Stretch Around
The Horizon
Cascading Drops
Of Moisture
Fill Her Mind

Sensations Light
The Desert
With Rambling Thoughts
As The Moon Fills
Itself
With Nectar

Pulsating Waves
Of Consciousness
Glow With Prayer
In Unorthodox Gestures
Known To God
But Unknown
Flickering Rainbows
Dazzle

The Sky
And
Kiss
The Clouds
Within
Her Reach

Nothing Sacred
Bounces
On Grounds
Of Airlessness
While Life Walks Casually
On
The Beach Of Dreams

Forging
An Implant
On The Steps
Of Nothing
Creation Toils
In The Web
Of Moments

Free Will

Effortlessly
I Move From One Life
To Another
My Waking World
Of Day Dreams
Ends
And Becomes
An Overwhelming
Land
Of Consciousness

Freely
I Fly
Or Run
Through This Vast Universe
Experiencing
Simultaneous Dimensions
That Pack Me
Into A Package
And Send Me
To The Doorstep
Of Infinity
Where I Ring
The Bell
Of Unity

Awakened
By the Connection
Of Creation
I Get Out Of Bed
To Dream Again

Consciousness Conforms

Intersecting Dreams
Build Physical Events
As Consciousness Conforms
In Unconformity

Massive Structures
Develop
Into Reality

Pyramids Stand
In Freedom
Praising Wisdom

A Sleeping World
Of Change
Brings Active Thoughts
To Form

Energy
Grips Itself
In Truth
Daily Life Becomes
The Dream
Of Angels

Walking Silently
Between The Pulsating
Vibration
I Open My Senses
To Feel Eternity

Through Selfhood
Consciousness Rings
A Chime
Of Awareness
Connecting Itself
In
Creation

Snowflakes

The Sound
Of A Snowflake
Echoes
Through Time
As It Finds A Place Of Peace

Frozen Shapes
Of Geometry
Transport Water
In Majestic Beauty
Filling Space
With Artistic Flair

The Simple Water Drop
Becomes
The Maestro
Of A Diverse Orchestra
Covering Life
With The Blanket
Of Energy
It Then Disappears
In A Bed
Of Mystery

Forever Present
In Conscious Thought
The Voice
Of Snowflake
Whispers My Name

Liquid Love

Freshly Painted Thoughts
Connect Realities
Fragments Of Consciousness
Are Joined
In Flowing Strokes
From The Master
Brush Of Unity

Hidden Landscapes
Color Themselves
In Splendor
Ancient Knowledge Speaks
In Fauna Voices
Animals
Become Proficient In Dialects
Insects
Build A New World Order
Birds
Fill Nests With Freedom

Seas
Engage In Communion
Earth
Finds Another Space
As Sun Spots Rage
Moons
Glow In Liquid Love
A Universal Language
Becomes Peace
Within Itself

Web Of Mobility

Gliding
Back And Forth
Between Selves
My World Becomes Stable

Reality Is No Longer
Singular
But A Triality
Vibrant Experiences
Are No Longer Expectations
But Actual

History Digests Itself
In An Aspect Self
Perceptions
Are No Longer Linear
But Multidimensional

Universal Thoughts
Become Transformational
Collective Consciousness
Mirrors
Abundant Possibilities

Feelings Connect Dimensions
Emotionally
Unconditionally
And
Gracefully

Love
Locks Waves
Of Thought
Energetically
In Twelve Dimensions
Of Totality

A Plethora
Of Majestic Artistry
Meshed
In A Web
Of Mobility
Created
Infinitely

Death

The Death
Of A Caterpillar
Is Life
To A Butterfly

Pure Consciousness
In Colors
Two Worlds Met
In The Unity
Of Creation

I Too
Am A Caterpillar
My Cells And Molecules Dying
Only
To Be Born Again
Fueled
By Energy
I Become
The Image
Of My Source

Dazzling Molecules
Arranged In Unison
Universal Thoughts
Are Unleashed Uniformly
Uninhibited Unions
Are
Unfettered By Freedom
Perceptions Unfold
In Undulatory Forms
Ungovernable Graciousness
Filters
Through My Body

Life Is Undeniable
In Its Power
Of Death

Holons

Complete Harmony
Lives
Within Me

Aspects
Of My Self
Are Connected
With Energy
And
Express Themselves
In Their Reality
As Well
As Mine

All
A Part
Of The Whole
Of My
Source Self

Old Answers
Are Useless
They Bounce
Off The Walls
Of New Questions
Falling Into A Cage
Of Ignorance
The Consciousness
Of Infinity
Flash And Blink
In

Multidimensional
Thoughts
My Linear Existence
Becomes Circular
Time and Space
Wander Freely
1 Inch Towards
My Mirror
And See
Holons
Of
My Self

Serenity Rules

Colors Of Peace
Glow
In Warm Waters
Of Consciousness
Misty Clouds Vaporize
In Forgiveness

Ancient Warriors
Tell A Different Tale
Past Upheavals
Rest
In Understanding

Future Probabilities
Engage In Freedom
Without Oppression

Now
Threads
The Needle
Of Time
Stitching Dreams
Into Reality
Faulty Genes Grow
Into
Giants
Of Mercy

Dirty Laundry
Cleans Itself
In Gratitude
Nimble Thoughts
Conquer Anger
Fear Dives
Into The Straight
Of Energy

Breathing Life
Into
The Strength
Of Free Will
Anxiousness Rides
Into the Sunset
With Judgment
In His Saddlebags

Angels
Are
The Government
Of Change
Serenity Rules
In Unity

I Will Know

The Spring Solstice
Brings Gifts

It Brings Remembering
To Life
In Remembering
I Will Know

I Will Know
My Prayers
Are Thoughts
Thoughts Become
Things

I Will Know
My God
Is Perfect
In All Names
In All Religions
There
Is One Perfection
That
Grows In Diversity

I Will Know
I Am
A Whole
That Is
Part
Of
A Greater Whole
A Whole
Of Perfection
That
Is Constantly Changing

I Will Know
What I See In Others
Is Me
Looking
Into A Mirror
Of Reflection

I Will Know
I Am Forgiveness
In Every Inch
Of Me

I Will Know
I Am Spirit
Molded
In The Shape
Of Matter

I Will Know
I Am Connected
To All Life
In All Forms
In
Harmony

I Will Know
I Was Born
To Know
That I Am God
Creating Me
In His Likeness

I Will Know
His Name
Of No Name
In The Eternal Stream
Of Consciousness

Expression

Within Matter
I Exist
To Create
And Experience

Pulsating Consciousness
Emits Energy
From
Clusters Of Families
To Express Life

Dancing Impulses
Set Off
A World of Probabilities
That Captivate
My Senses

Freely Choosing
My Probabilities
I Evoke
The Will
Of Determination
And Connection
To Lead Me
In
An Linear Illusion

Wandering
To Remember Myself
I Grow In Spirit
Yet

Have Always
Been Grown
I Open
The Door
Of Possibilities
And
See Myself
Engaged
In Artistic Revival
With Other Aspects
Of Love

Reality
Is Plural
And
My
Dimensional Awareness
Is
Interchangable

With Change
Comes
The Essence
Of Being One
With
All Expression

My Circle Of Beauty

My Circle Of Beauty
Glows
With The Colors
Of Eternity

Like The Rose
I Bloom
Into
Petals
Of Life

Each Petal
A World Of Perfection
A Perfect Part
Of A Perfect Whole
Is What
I Am

Like The Rose
Drinking
The Raindrops
Of Awareness
I'm Connected
To Roots Of Giving
To Branches Of Gratitude
And
Thorns Of Protection

I Bask
In The Glow Of Light
And Dream
In The Mist
Of Darkness
Awakening
To A New Perception

I Create
New Life
Within Me

I Expand
In Awe
Of My Creation
And Die

Just To Bloom Again
In My Circle
Of
Oneness

Emergence

Locked
In Three Dimensional Reality
A Key Appears
Within Me
A Fluid Thought
Of Escape
Flows Freely

Empathy
Fills My Stream
Of Consciousness
And A Pure Eminence
Of Feeling
Immerses Me
In Unknown
Knowing

Emergent
Discoveries Appear
My Body Emigrates
Acquiescently

It's Acquittal
Is
A Whiff Of Freshness
From
An Old Acquaintance
In
The Vastness

Of Dimensions

Emphatic Vibrations
Meet
in An Emporium
Of Love

My Empirical Formula
Of Life
Has No Elements
But Empowers
My Emotions
With
Emergence

Perceptions

I Look Up
To Look Within
Conditioning
Has Left Its Imprints
On My Mind

My Directions
Are Set By My Perceptions
So Neatly Compacted
Into A Small Aspect
Of My
Consciousness

My Small Figure Of Matter
Emerges
My Entity Is Created
By Multidimensional Thoughts
That Move Within
Time And Space

I Try To Remember
My Other Selves
As They Waltz In And Out
Of My Perceptions
A Group Of Selves Invisible
To My Senses
But Alive
In My Consciousness
What Self

Shall I Meet Today
What Wisdom
Shall I Embrace
How Will I Share
My Love

Being Is My Grace
I Am Within
The Conscious Grid Of Infinity
My Perceptions
Glow As I Grow
Time and Space
Is Just One Place
Where The Gift Of Love
Overflows
In Choices

A Connected Awareness

Captivating Laughter
Is
The Face Of Love
It Drips Between
The Crevices Of Knowing
Each Giggle Rings
A Bell of Freedom

Vibrations
Match Themselves
In Numbers
Crossing
The Vastness Of Nothing
In Synchronicity
Carrying DNA
In Mystical Strands
Of Being

A Connected Awareness
Kisses Itself
In Dreams
Falling
Into The Well
Of Oneness

Embracing
The Essence
Of Remembering
The Dance
Of Friendship
Begins
Where It Left Off

Holding Love
In Magic Memories
And Moments
In Absolute Bliss

Dripping In Delight
The Energy
Of Consciousness
Brings
Thoughts
To Life
And
Purpose
To Love

The Mode

Shall I Be
A Flower
Or
A Tree
A Lake
Or
Mountain
Or The Planet
That Holds Them
I Must See Them
As
Me Consciously

There Is No Other Reality
If My Focus Rests
In Pure Quantum Diversity
I Can Be
Any Probability

What I See
Changes Worlds
In Me

Energy Waves
In Fluid Artistry
Particles Dance
With
Flowing Multiplicity
Matter Dines
With Believability
Parallel Dimensions
Find Actuality

Within Me Sits
Complexity
Resting
In A Divine Web
Of Possibilities

Shall I Be
The God
In Me

Imagination
Paves
The Road

Life
Is
The Mode

IN

In
Contrast There
Is Growth

In
Belief There
Is Faith

In
Thought There
Is Creation

In
Consciousness There
Is Multiplicity

In
Dreams There
Is Healing

In
Matter There
Is Illusion

In
Life There
Is Continuity

In
God There
Is Laughter

In
Love There
Is Energy

In
Me There
Is
All There Is

About The Author

Howard (Hal) Thomas Manogue, was born in Philadelphia, and is a forerunner to the Indigo children, a now age term for misfit with an intuitive nature, a desire to know his truth with a gift of giving and sharing. Hal retired from the shoe industry after 35 years of sole searching, and discovered his real soul. He enjoys art, music, philosophy, psychology, nature and people.

Hal started writing poetry in 1996. His first book: Short Sleeves A Book For Friends, was self-published in 2003. His second book; Short Sleeves A Book For Friends 2006 Collection, was released in May 2006. His third book the 2007 collection of Short Sleeves was released in January 2007. The 2008 Collection was released in July 2008

His poems have been published by: Mystic Pop Magazine, Children Of The New Earth Magazine, New Age Tribune, Seasons Of The Soul Newsletters, The Ascension Network, Lightship News, New World View, and Writers In The Sky Newsletters. His essays can be found on www.ezinearticles. com, and www.authorsden.com, www.jasonsnetwork.com , www.godblesshumanity.com As well as his blog:
 http://halmanogue.blogspot.com/
He lives in Franklin Tennessee.

Hal's new book: "Short Sleeves Insights: Live An Ordinary Life In A Non-Ordinary Way" was released in May 2008. Essays from the book have already been published in books and newsletters around the globe.

For More Information visit: www.shortsleeves.net or http://halmanogue.blogspot.com/ email: hal at shortsleeves.net